Darkhaired

Olive Broderick

Templar Poetry

First Published 2010 by Templar Poetry
Templar Poetry is an imprint of Delamide & Bell

Fenelon House
Kingsbridge Terrace
58 Dale Road, Matlock, Derbyshire
DE4 3NB
www.templarpoetry.co.uk

ISBN 978-1-906285-93-7

A CIP catalogue record of this book is available from the British Library.

Typeset by Pliny
Cover: lino cut by James Weir
Printed and bound in India

For my sisters

Acknowledgements

Thanks are due to the editors of the following journals and anthologies who first published some of these poems, or versions of them: *West 47/Cúirt Annual 2005* ('Darkhaired'); *Sunday Tribune* ('Market Forces' and 'Misconception'); *Ulla's Nib* ('Solstice at Killard'); *Tinteán Magazine* ('Lament of the Wandering Worker'); *The Stinging Fly* ('A poem only in Translation).

'Market Forces' and Misconception' were chosen as winning poems of the Hennessy X.O Literary Award, Emerging Poetry Category 2009. 'Darkhaired' was a finalist in the Cúirt International Festival of Literature 2005 *New Writing Prize*.

Acknowledgement is due to the Arts Council of Northern Ireland for their support of work produced in 2009.

The majority of these poems were written between 2007-2009. Much thanks is due to facilitators and members of QUB Writer's Group, Write! Down members, family and friends for their encouragement and sound advice during this time.

Thanks to Carrie Etter for her considerable help and support.

Contents

Darkhaired

(Cello Concerto O.58 – Prokofiev)

A stormy night finally ends in squally
showers with intermittent sunshine.
A fretful dream of being instrumental.
The instrument of a musician who
approaches a composer cautiously,
courting, not directly asking for
a composition. A trainer with a colt
who is close to breaking. All the while
talking about other things –
like the tone and colour of some phrasing
or the state, at the time, of all things Russian.
His patience is rewarded, finally, with this.
Turbulent, it must be tightly conducted.
A rough crossing – though there are calmer moments.
I feel your presence in the playing out of this.
Feel you close and the fractured lines of melody
are a chaos in my mind – all broken
up and moving, unable to grasp the rules of it.
Holding on so tightly that I assume
your scent, and I do not want it to end.

Note

Mo lon dubh
you are far away from home
Tone for me
a single line from some old lay -
A lost tale
of one who thought that gorse was gold

Your head
held high
and I

Half-hypnotized draw pictures
Of what I hope will be there
When this mist clears
Even if it is as I predict
A width of water still
Lies between us and
The far shore

(lon dubh – blackbird)

Lament for those on Epic Journeys

You catch the grace notes as they fall,
holding your voice steady against the wind,
a heavy mist off the Atlantic.
Salt on your lips, melody unmade by the gale.

Even by mistake, words held back
or left for too long unsaid
become imprisoned inside,
forever planning their escape.

Arduous journeys. Mourne's moat of cloud
traversed to scale the petrol blue against
cornflower, and on the other side the sheer drop to
offset *that* colour in yet another register.

Or further off to deep within the desert:
garments of the travel weary slipped off and
left suspended on an old-fashioned clothes horse
among the drying blankets of a Bedouin camp.

Always the moon; and a lighthouse on the far shore
which mimics its course but is too perfect in its rotation.
An undetected wave reaches further forward than the last
but is caught by the undertow and forced to withdraw.

Rana Road

Were you singing? Don't Stop.
Yes, we know the danger of all this wet weather
and we've learned the cataclysmic names of that
which accompanies earthquakes and hurricanes:
and the nonsense of burying waste in separate places,
and petrol, household detergents, industrial chemicals,
all brought together by rising water levels;
and bad timing which sees more rain fall where
there is already more than enough water.
Then the fact that pollution diluted is still poisonous,
the damage which is so indelible and the endless
waiting for decisions on whether levees should be repaired,
when it's clear that they shouldn't ever have been there.
This is no time for Bore Hole Monster stories,
it is no longer children who need telling.
I remember a hot day in Miranda de Ebro in the early '90s,
reaching to quench my thirst at what I thought
was a drinking fountain; and a local who caught the lever first,
pointing firmly, at a sign which read: AGUA NON POTABLE

I remember, too, Miranda the following February,
as if you were present, magical, though I think we told you later
about how the street that we lived on got its nickname.
It is midnight, there is moonlight and a recent deluge
has left a layer of pebbles on Calle San Nicolas. *'Look'*
our Spanish friend says. *'Ranas. What do you call them in English?'*
We stare at the silver puddles and see, to our surprise,
a pebble hops sideways and then another; and train our eyes
on the nearby river bank which seems to be vibrating.
He explains to us this yearly occurrence and we make a game
of who gets to the front door first without stepping on one.
Then we begin to debate, laughing, whether it would be worse
to be disturbed or to die in coitus. And then there is silence
among us because if we are honest this sight is stirring;
then the sound: swollen, heavy, systolic. Singular.
Each one answering the call of its own nature.
Absurd magnificent this potent augur,
the ancient foretelling of the Spring Rains.
Were *you* singing? Don't Stop.

Étude for the Left

on hearing Ivan Llic play Godowsky's Chopin arrangements

This close night. The town clock
won't chime the hour. The windows
all shut tight as if the music
were outside. Somewhere else
in this house you are at the piano
practising a variation on a Chopin
lullaby. Becoming phrase perfect
and I can hear how you have been
rising to take my place, drawing
into your domain those things
about me that please you most,
retreating deep into your own region,
lost in the contented melancholy
of all this and, undisturbed,
you have set your centre of gravity
so that it can support one only.
The rain has come and I curl
into myself, a question turned
in on itself, my redundant
notes of rose and jasmine.

Son et Lumière

Alas
At times
I find
Exquisite bitterness
In
Your Kiss.
(Rudolph Valentino, extract ***Day Dreams***)

It's all so fragile: like fine bone china
for a child's tea-set. The clock stops ticking,
days run on unchecked, still calling your name
which means *dream-come-true*. But unrealised,
pretend that it's fine. Should I be the one
to say what I want? I feel my longing.
If you come again, will I be immune
because I know now: or return once more
- spectral and moving in time to music -
to the pale island between screen and here
where no-one, truly, speaks to each other.

Diane's Sitter

There came a moment that you couldn't tell.
And then they clearly flew instead of fell.
- Howard Nemerov

Don't say Die-, *it's* Dee-*Ann*. My mother's voice comes before every introduction; and my childhood home. All of us standing, perfectly turned out for inspection by guests. *This wonderful house, such beautiful children. How do you do it, Mrs Nemerov*. My mother's shoulders drop, imperceptibly. *Go and play, now, children*. But we had stopped playing like that. We withdraw to an out-of-the-way room, more sparsely decorated, but no less tasteful. Howard sits with a book or his pencils, me on the cosy window box watching. Even the little one, who I used to chide with – *remember what Mother said* or *think of Daddy's clients,* is lost in a magical union of herself and her crayons.

This morning my head is full of memories. *Isn't that Alan Arbus' wife? Did she leave him? Those strange photographs*. I am out walking with my camera. It's not a dog, but the strap seems to pull in my hand as if the eagerness doesn't come entirely from me. I am ambling about this park but there is nothing to see here. There is nothing to draw my eye or make the hard casing of the camera warm in my hands. Disappointed. *Don't be like that Diane, most people wish they had what you have.* Turning to leave:

I see her, sitting on a park bench. I feel a shock of recognition. Maybe she is one of my mother's friends. My hands fly to my throat, automatically self-conscious that I have left the house without washing, hair uncombed, picking fluff from yesterday's sweater. She looks at me, startled, as though she thinks she has seen me somewhere before too. She is younger than I thought. Maybe she was a client of our photographic studio. Alan would remember.

I move forward, introduce myself without names and, no, it's clear we don't know each other. She asks, politely, about the camera. I ask, politely, if I may take a photograph and she answers with her hands. One moves upwards, slightly, indicating the worry of a stray in the lacquered hair, or her choker gone awry, and the other moves in the direction of the hem of her tailored skirt, and beyond to the handbag where it will find a jewelled mirror. But I cut short the journey. *It's not that kind of photograph – be as you were.*

She is the ideal sitter. She neither regards nor disregards the camera. Her eyes follow me for a short time, while I and the camera's view finder compose a picture of an unknown woman sitting alone on a park bench: sad today. It is over quickly. I am so grateful to her. I know I am a stranger. I am walking away quickly, always longing to see what will develop, always convinced that it will turn out true to my perception. I can't remember whether I have thanked her, exchanged the last pleasantries, or whether I walked away without saying anything.

The Oakwood Trilogy

1. *His Child*

He asks me to bear his child.
No gold ring accurately measured
could fit so constantly as what
he asks me. After he makes
his request he leaves the room.
Our appointment is over.
Quietly behind him, the door
closes.

2. *Bathwater*

I do not feel safe with you in my arms.
Like branches they are weak
and we are disproportionate.
Your head is heavy and fragile
and your neck is delicate.
You make a dent in the curve
of my arm. I cannot hold you up.
I sink, and the water closes over us like
a lid.

3. *The Weeping Woman*

Please don't leave so quickly.
As terrible as this appears to be –
it's only an old water fountain
trying for one last time to flow.
First coughing up the silt and
rotten flora of seasons of disuse,
then washing away the outer dirt.
Once the duct is re-opened,
these tears must spill
over.

Market Forces

Tonight, love, the moon is big over Drake's Pool
and the wood on the far bank is clearly defined
in shadow. The air is so clear that I can hear
the faint '*ching, ching, ching*' of the breeze against
the masts of the yachts that are moored there.
There is too much sweetness about all this.

Tomorrow everything will be as normal.
All of that has been organised already.
The school run, the groceries, the monthly payments
- all confidently sorted. Nothing to do now
but figure out how best to tell the children.

When I get home, I imagine, we will talk
'til well past midnight, trying to read between
the lines of a far-off dissertation; and how
the turn of a page can have such disastrous
consequences. But still, hearing in our minds
the voices of our parents, repeat assurances
of how this might well bring something better.

And in the small hours glad to have each other,
whispering, where will we be this time next year?

Social Dance

for Mr & Mrs Egan

Dervishes open themselves to God
but here they hold each other as if

their arms are the closed loop of an
electronic circuit that carries

a compound core-to-core which broken
- down will always yield a different

composition; where the traditional
molding of leader and follower

has rubbed away through constant motion.
Many of the adept steer clear of

the faux pas of nervous beginners;
but there are some who leave their other,

briefly, to offer an invitation
to a novice, lead her to the floor,

gifting her a touch of what can be
though the steps he chooses are far too

simple to sustain his interest.
Afterwards they admire each other

– him for his mastery, her for her
willingness to join in the social

talk of bodies. I remember that;
and back-sliding. I finger the bars

of my prison- trapezius,
quadriceps femoris, gastrocne-

mius, no time – of which the last is
the most urgent. I must find a partner.

We must climb the four to one gradient
to where the city moves below –

sensous at nightime – as if it
is two cities held apart and

reconnected by a series of
bridges that stretch across the river.

Burrow

(on watching investigations of child abuse at Haut de Garenne, Jersey
& after three poems by Gabriela Mistral)

They do not like that I dance alone.
I embrace this. I open my arms

to you who are beyond reach - deeply
buried – from whom nobody has heard;
to you who may have emigrated;
you who quietly self-medicate,
somewhere else, but always well turned out
so that there is no need to guess that
you had once believed you'd rule your world.

I embrace you, as once I nestled
so close to someone whose scent remains
in my air, in memory. For whom
I would happily face the echoing
cavern of the minotaur to see
again. Empty and silent, I turn
automatic revolutions, forgetting.
where I am. Aware this must look strange
and the space in my arms is ice-cold.

Embrace this. Don't assume it's because
I have done something wrong; dig deeper.

Solstice at Killard

The sun sets late leaving behind
Washed out streaks of pinks and browns
Leaving behind a sickly kind of light

The temperature drops almost immediately
And the group spreads waterproof coverings
Over the damp grass of the sand-dunes

Three of us head to the sea two to swim and I to wade
in the shallow water as if it was a summer evening
At Whiting Bay Caliso Bay or Clay Castle

Where we would walk the length of the beach
Talking or just aware of the release pause
Recoil pause of the small waves under our feet

Behind me they are splashing about
And the sound of giggling carries me
Back to the narrow strip of sand and rocks

Behind the wall of our town where we would attempt
To go from the Coast Guard Station to the Front Strand
By the edge of the Blackwater as much as possible

Wise enough to never do this alone
Wily in avoiding the advance of tides or failing light
Knowing well why this route was forbidden

Instinctively, I scan the horizon
Out of the blur unfamiliar lights on the far shore
And the contours of dunes flattened to black

I have no idea where I am

Disoriented and agitated by my own stupidity
I turn back and even when re-united with the others
I am still feeling unexpectedly and completely lost

By the time we return the group are fractious
And they haven't lit a fire and want to go home
It takes awhile to gather up everything

Behind our backs the moon comes up
Ember-red then cooling to rose-gold
As it rises slowly over the water

Lament of the Wandering Worker

Of waterfalls and still clear water -
somewhere on the banks of the Murray River
we search the night sky of the Southern Hemisphere
for stars that are familiar.

There by chance, I meet someone like him
and once again my heart is ripped
like a page carefully torn at a fold in its centre –
once again the 'nays' find favour.

The Herons of Harty's Quay

A heron flies over the footbridge -
charcoal line against the darkening sky.

On the far bank, the apartment complex is lit from below
and sparkles like Mary's *Mont St Michel at Evening.*

At an unmarked place beyond the plaque remembering
someone who drowned here, and the remains of an old pier

two herons land and appear to sit as a couple on the river:
their long outlines steady in the wavering grey of the current.

Colour retreats completely and, now, instead of chiming six;
some bell rings out '*Abide with me*'.

Three herons rise above the estuary.
Shadows in the air; shadows on the water.

2 November 2008

Leabharcham sleeps

She will scold when she discovers I have opened wide the shutters
and am standing in my night gown only, in the frame of the window,
with the air current that stirs the snowflakes into a mist around me,
catching my linen shift so that I feel that I am part of the blizzard.
I am wide awake for brightness. I was not expecting it this morning.

I have spent so much time at this window, watching, that now they ask me
to predict the weather. I have witnessed how gold light at the edge
of the clearest sky means a frost will follow later. One shade of grey cloud
means rain that falls all day without ceasing, another tells of rain
that threatens without falling. But I am not certain about snow.

Once in Autumn, when I was still a child, I asked her to tell me about it.
When she replied that it was white and soft, I touched the ermine lining
of the stole he had given me for my birthday. She answered, yes, but
it is not warm. It is cold as the stone of our turret, unrelieved cold
like the forehead of your dead mother. And he had silenced her -

saying there are things that should not be mentioned in front of children.
And when I grasped the fur in one hand and with the other stroked
the unyielding flagstones of the wall of this room, he smiled and said,
almost, but unlike stone, snow is frozen water which returns to molten
when it encounters something which has a higher temperature.

Since then snow has come and lain beyond my window. But this is the first time I have felt it. It is warmer than I expected. Then, quite suddenly, the tossed sheet returns to the ground to settle, to make a new landscape of the landscape with which I am familiar. Even the garrison wall looks less forbidding. There is a different kind of quiet.

And the colours that re-appear are intense in contrast. The sky, now azure and gleaming, gazes down direct so that I lower my eyes and my face reddens. A raven, deep-black, lands on the sill. Its feathers thick, shining, and I want to draw my fingers through them. My heart beats in anticipation. The bird flies out of reach when I reach out to touch it.

Leaning out, as far as I am able, what I feel is longing. Longing for the stone wall of the tower to be snow - snow that melts when my warm body presses against it. And once free of its constraint then longing to lay the length of myself, white on white, the snow molding slightly to contain my shape but compacting, also, so as to remain.

And I am trembling though I feel no cold, not from the snow, nor from the stones I lean my full weight against, not even from being close to naked in late winter. And it is my experience that one event precedes another, for myself, as for the weather. But here I cannot guess the sequence. I will wake Leabharcham and ask her what this means.

Misconception

This is a poem about a moon
that was visible one clear day
in December: three quarters visible -
buttermilk against delphinium -
as framed in a pane of this window:
and a sequence of airplanes
with short contrails, swimming
through the blue, in its direction,
particularly the first seemed sure
to merge with the stationary orb –
but missed it by what looked like
little more that a millimetre.

In this Seraglio

There may not always be a need for exile.
I may not always be so silent. It is morning.
Once-warm silks have lost their shape and been replaced –
tulips that wilted in last night's heat
allargando.

The sun this morning dazes, making everyone
too bright or dark. From a hidden recess I watch
a guest of this house address a crowd. Letting him fade,
caught in the cross-fire, between two
melodies.

He is singing too. Or so it seems through my veil.
Less easily drawn aside than a curtain of pearls,
or the purple jade I wear for dénouement.
I may not always be so silent. He has not
stopped,

and I am thinking, relating things to those,
not present, in the language of their understanding -
forgetting, for a moment anyhow, that the flowers
have died - and they are still far from hearing.

on hearing Yang Lian read
'A night at the purple tulip palace (adagio)'

A poem only in translation

(after the Eastern European poet who refused to read her poem in its original language)

A pillowbook of veils and Autumn evenings.
A litany of all the loveliest things.
This lullaby that I will not sing to you
because I cannot watch you slip into a reverie
brought on by the sound of the words of this.

Hear instead a translation of the poem
which I wrote one Summer before the war.
I was in my then-kitchen making jam
with the window open onto a darkening sky
and I had a vision, had I known it then,
of how the streets of this place would soon
turn a deeper shade than any
Valentine's berry.

Have you ever loved anyone, maybe more than one
whereby even a hint of that foreshadowing
would cause a glass jar to slip from your hand
and shatter so badly that it can never be put back
together again.

Perhaps my retelling is inadequate.
But I cannot let you succumb to foreign words
whose sound without meaning might be like
a caress of waves at evening time or
a slow air on a finely tuned instrument.

Rapunzel

After the last let down I grew my hair – longer and blonder –
a strong statement that this time was different.
Instead, I walled myself in, to become steady, to mend.
Outside, I brazenly wore my hair up, like a woman
with intimates before whom she loosens it appropriately.
Alone, with my back to an upstairs window, the coiled braid is
undone.
I dry it until it lies about me in the imitation of an embrace
or as an invitation in a sealed envelope.

Hamadryad *or*
The Abandoned Garden

In the garden of the Rodin Museum,
at the midpoint of a linden avenue
where the upper branches conspire to shelter
visitors from the intense midday heat as
they move between *The Thinker* and the still pool
which has *Ugolino* at its centre,
a little girl in a sundress twists around
and around one tree, her left hand hooked
to its dark trunk; by herself in the shade,
a dark-haired child in a bright, white dress:
an old-fashioned negative that calls to be
developed over and over again.